EARTH'S HIDDEN
ANGELS

Janice Bell

BALBOA.
PRESS
A DIVISION OF HAY HOUSE

Balboa Press books may be ordered through booksellers or by contacting:

Balboa Press
A Division of Hay House
1663 Liberty Drive
Bloomington, IN 47403
www.balboapress.com
1 (877) 407-4847

Because of the dynamic nature of the Internet, any web addresses or links contained in this book may have changed since publication and may no longer be valid. The views expressed in this work are solely those of the author and do not necessarily reflect the views of the publisher, and the publisher hereby disclaims any responsibility for them.

The author of this book does not dispense medical advice or prescribe the use of any technique as a form of treatment for physical, emotional, or medical problems without the advice of a physician, either directly or indirectly. The intent of the author is only to offer information of a general nature to help you in your quest for emotional and spiritual well-being. In the event you use any of the information in this book for yourself, which is your constitutional right, the author and the publisher assume no responsibility for your actions.

Any people depicted in stock imagery provided by Thinkstock are models, and such images are being used for illustrative purposes only.
Certain stock imagery © Thinkstock.

Printed in the United States of America.

ISBN: 978-1-4525-9664-8 (sc)
ISBN: 978-1-4525-9665-5 (e)

Library of Congress Control Number: 2014907341

Balboa Press rev. date: 5/9/2014

DEDICATION

I dedicate this book to my daughter Sadie. To all the men and
women who have served and are serving our country today,
I say "Thank you." I also dedicate this poem to each and everyone
of our veterans. Dedicated to my dear friend Carolyn Kersey.

REBIRTH

Stroll through paths of tall trees, its leafs laden
with tiny droplets of dew at each tip.
The untainted air is refreshing with floral aromas of
wild flowers, honeysuckle and babys breath.
Rainbows circle the crystal clear lake, waterfalls
calling from afar to offer a cool dip.
Sunsets color the sky yellow, orange red purple and blue.
Flickering of amber flames overwhelm fire
is taking away all that we know.
Rebirth of life is taking store despite the charred black hole.
Amongst the ashen darkness a small ray of color emerges.
The only thing that has grown more are the souls that view.

Jamie Zel Blount

FOREWORD

This book is being written for therapeutic awareness and to bring the public on an enlighten journey giving them a perspective on the development of Depression with Anxiety and Panic Attacks without Agoraphobia through one persons trials and tribulations. Also revealed is Post Traumatic Stress Disorder. PTSD will be told for one civilian and one military man who spent eight years in the military and eighteen months fighting in Afghanistan. This young gentleman goes by the name Sergeant James.

Beginning with a clean slate, you will be introduced to a three-year-old child, through her adolescence as a young woman and last, a grown woman in her late fifties.

The trials and tribulations of Rhonda s life has lead to the above diagnosis which needs to be addressed so others will not be alarmed thinking they are the only victims of this and related illness' and situations. The main character, Rhonda, will give insight by revealing her life's events. Sergeant James will give you the perspective through a soldier's life in and off the battlefield and to explain exactly when his PTSD began and what he is doing to cope with this illness. This book is not to diagnose any situation outside of the main character, or Sergeant James.

I do hope the context of this book will share comfort, compassion, laughter and most of all knowledge with insight so you, the reader can grasp the meaning no matter how bad the situation is something good can come from it, allowing you to go forward with your head held high with dignity.

I strongly encourage you to get reliable counseling and know that there is treatment for PTSD. Help is just a phone call away. It is time we now take responsibility to care for our men and women in uniform who fought and laid down their lives for us.

Families send their sons, brothers, grandsons, daughters, granddaughters and sisters off to war. They come home to us as military brothers and sisters lost in a world that loud noises make them look over their shoulders and duck for cover. Our fighting loved one's are still numb, inside from battle. The purpose of this book is to let them and civilians know there is a way we can coupe and live without fear or have to look over our shoulders or shut those out that we love because they do not understand. The answer is therapy, counseling, psychologist, and psychiatrist; these are Earth's Hidden Angel's. Please seek out your hidden angel.

Janice Bell
Author

CHAPTER 1

Memories are recalled at various ages, sometimes triggered by a touch, scent, taste, sound and even a familiar scene. Let me introduce to you Rhonda, a blond with, hazel eyes, three year old whose recollection includes all five senses in her first childhood memory. The year was 1957. The place was,Baton Rouge, Louisiana.

Alfred Place was a long winding street with manicured lawns, blocked hedges leading to the front porch. The front windows had green-stripped awnings which shaded the morning and afternoon sun. Almost all of the porches had wooden swings swaying in the breeze. Rhonda's house was the fourth on the right.

In Baton Rouge, it is customary to call your parents' best friends Aunt and Uncle. Aunt Louise and Uncle Eddie lived next door. Rhonda's Mother and Father both worked Monday through Friday. Rhonda spent those hours with Aunt Louise and Uncle Eddie.

Rhonda's day began at the back screen door of Aunt Louise's kitchen. "Good Morning," Rhonda would say. Aunt Louise, opening the screen door would ask, "Do you want to have toast and coffee with me?" Rhonda replied, "Yes, please!"

Aunt Louise's kitchen was filled with aromas of fresh brewed coffee, which sat on the back right burner of her gas stove. As she opened the oven door to get our toast, baked ham mingled with the coffee and toast and it was heavenly.

As the curtains swayed over the kitchen table, Rhonda moved the softened butter away from the window. Aunt Louise would make "special coffee" for Rhonda. A mixture of coffee and condensed milk; tasted better than any candy Rhonda ever had. Lets not forget the toast with homemade strawberry jam dripping off the golden crispy edges.

After the dishes were washed and the potatoes peeled, Aunt Louise would turn the radio on. The all to familiar voice of Paul Harvey filled every room of the house.

Aunt Louise's chores seemed never ending. We went outside and took the clothes off the line. Rhonda would place the clothes in the basket. While waiting for the next arm full, Rhonda would feel the clover in between her toes. It was a soft cushiony feeling and cool to the touch. Aunt Louise had her ironing board, starch and a soda pop bottle filled with water with a sprinkler top all set to fold and iron the clean laundry in her bedroom. As Rhonda watched Aunt Louise hard at workRhonda's eye's began to close. It was the ideal place to nap. The window was open and the breeze softly whipped across the bed cooling the room. The smell of freshly ironed clothes over powered the smell of ham.

Rhonda woke to the sound of birds chirping out side and the smell of pine sol in the air. After Aunt Louise finished her chores she would set at the kitchen table and enjoy a cup of her special coffee.

Ronda ate lunch and then went outside to play. Time passed by quickly. Rhonda had a routine every day. Rhonda would walk up and down the driveway waiting to see Uncle Eddie's truck. At the first glimpse Rhonda ran to the garage to wait for Uncle Eddie to pull up in the driveway. With opened arms he walked towards her and picks her up. Kisses on the cheek and Rhonda asked, "Are you ready?" Uncle Eddie would reply, "You bet!"

Every day when Uncle Eddie came home from work he would go straight to the garage. Walking into the garage, to the left was a huge sink. Rhonda would get a bath in there when she got to muddy to go inside. Next to the sink were the washer and (2) two refrigerators. The first one belonged to Uncle Eddie. It was filled with Jax beer. The beer was so cold it had slivers of ice in the first few sips. Rhonda was allowed to open the can with the church key hanging by the garage door. To this day, Rhonda will stick a beer or two in the freezer and wait with anticipation for that first icy sip. Uncle Eddie had to stay outside as long as he was drinking his beer. Aunt Louise did not allow it in the house.

Aunt Louise was superstitious. On Fridays, if you came in the back door you must leave through the back door.

Rhonda never understood if this was due to her religious belief or if it was her rule. Needless to say, Rhonda knew the consequences if the rule was broken; something bad would happen to you, so Rhonda followed Aunt Louises' every wish.

Rhonda's house had a fenced in yard to keep Rhonda and her dog, Douty from roaming the neighborhood. Douty and Rhonda had a secret hiding place, under the house behind the stairs leading into the kitchen. Rhonda and Douty would share doggie biscuits in the hiding place. Rhonda's favorite line was, "One for you and one for me." Rhonda had one other special place; only this one was just for her and it was inside her house.

Rhonda had two older sisters and one older brother. Bobbie was seventeen years old, Betty was thirteen years old and her older brother, Douglas, was fourteeen. Bobbie and Douglas were upset with one another, and Douglas picked Bobbie up and threw her through the wall. Literally. As Bobbie climbed out of the hole she had made in the wall, Rhonda climbed in and before anyone noticed, all her toys were in the hole as well. A new toy box and play area. Rhonda did not mind the lack of playing with other children her own age. Her life was filled with love and imagination.

Rhonda's Daddy called her inside one afternoon. Rhonda and Douty climbed out from under the house and went in side to see what her Daddy wanted. "Yes sir", said Rhonda to her Daddy. "Please remove all your toys from your special place in the hall for me." Rondaa's Daddy asked. Rhonda replied, "Yes sir." Uncle Eddie came over. He and Daddy patched the hole in the wall.

Rhonda was going for rides with her Mother and Daddy to see a very large and thick slab of concrete with pipes sticking out of it. The most exciting thing was a big pile of sand. Rhonda would end up in the sand even if she had a dress on. Each time they visited it looked more like a big house, which she learned later was going to be her new home. All of Rhonda's family was rushing about placing their belongings into boxes. That same week, Rhonda went home and got the dog biscuits, and started looking for Douty. He was nowhere to be found. Rhonda told her Mother she could not find Douty.

Her Mother said, "The gate was left open when they where taking boxes out to the truck and Douty ran away." Rhonda's head hung very low and her heart was cracked open. Soon it was time to say "Good Bye" to Aunt Louise and Uncle Eddie. This too was very hard. Rhonda would not see them again until she was in her mid teens.

Rhonda thought of Aunt Louise and Uncle Eddie often and as for Douty, she still remembers him and hopes he found a good home. Now Rhonda has a new home, no pets, and no friends but a big yard to explore.

A young child at this age who just lost her dog and her Aunt and Uncle has definite psychological effects especially if there is not adult communication. The brother and sisters were already old enough to understand what was going on but Rhonda was in the dark with no explanation except she had a new house. Moving is devastating enough, but to lose the routine of everyday life for a young person is very confusing and possibly can lead to long-term problems later in life.

CHAPTER 2

Rhonda learned why she went on frequent rides to the thick cement square with pipes sticking out of it. Rhonda was in the car with her Father and Mother, which lead the moving van with all their belongings inside. As the car pulled into the driveway there was now a pink brick house sitting on the cement slab. The sand pile was gone. The grass was thick and freshly cut all around the house. "This is our new home." Rhonda's mother replied. "Let's go see inside." Rhonda did not know what to think. It was so much bigger than the house she just left. Walking inside she was told, "This is the den where we will watch T.V. "Rhonda saw a big wood paneled room with sliding glass doors facing a porch outside. All the floors were hard and shiny with dots, black and brown. Her Mother explained the floor was called terrazzo.

The next room was the kitchen with sliding glass doors leading to the porch outside same as the den. Then came the living room. The only room with carpet a dark blue and a mural on the right side of the room. It was beautiful; tall trees with a path each side filled with ferns leading to a waterfall and clear pond. The top was the most beautiful blue skyline with clouds that looked so real they seemed to flow. The front door was in this room. To the left was a doorway leading to the long hall. At each end was a bedroom. To the right, there was a bathroom and two more bedrooms. At the far end to the left was a bathroom for the master bedroom. It was a big house. The hall was great for sock skating.

Before she knew it,Rhonda's Grandmother, Nannie moved in. Nannie was Rhonda's Mother's Mother. Rhonda was happy her Nannie was going to live with them. Nannies bedroom was in the front of the house. Her sewing machine went with her wherever she was. She sewed beautiful ballroom dresses and ball gowns for grown-ups and dresses and aprons for Rhonda.

Nannie painted China dolls and she also made the bodies and stuffed them with cotton. Then she dressed them each with a different dress that she had made, one for each girl in the house. Rhonda's had red hair and she wore a yellow gown with 3 petticoats. Rhonda was very careful not to let her feet touch together because they could chip easily. They were made to sit on our beds after making it each morning. After the beds were made no one was allowed to sit or lie on them until it was time for bed. Nannie would get upset if anyone sat on the beds after they were made.

Rhonda had a lot of exploring to do. There was a big lot next to us that led into the woods. Rhonda picked berries and found neat new bugs under wood and rocks. Rhonda was picking blackberries, big ones, to give to Nannie and saw a red and black long thing. She picked at it with a stick and it jumped up scaring her so bad she dropped her berries and ran home. Rhonda was yelling for help because the snake was chasing her. Rhonda did not know they did that. Rhonda's Daddy came out of the Den door and asked what she had found. Rhonda told him a snake and Daddy said he was probably gone by now. Rhonda looked at him as she ran passed him and asked, "Is there something red and black following me?" Daddy said, "Yes! Oh, I'll go get your brother. Run in the house Rhonda." Douglas came out the door and the snake was on the carport. He was curled up in the corner as if he were waiting for me to go back out and play with him. Rhonda went to her room. This way Rhonda did not have to see what the end result was. Rhonda had decided to stay inside for a while after the snake ordeal.

After Rhonda cut up all the Sears and Roebuck catalogues, for her paper dolls, she decided it was time to go back outside. Rhonda met up with a crawfish. She remembered you could cook them, but these where living in the ditch across the street from her house. Needless to say, Nannie did not take to kindly to the fact that her granddaughter was playing in the ditch. Nannie's famous line was, "Rhonda, you are going to catch diphtheria!" "Get out of that ditch now or you will regret it." Nannie made Rhonda cut her own switch and if it was to small it had to be replace. In the spring, when the new limbs were emerging, it was wooden spoon time. Nannie did mean business. Rhonda could not have loved any one more than her Nannie and Daddy and Mother.

Rhonda looked forward to Saturday. This was the day Daddy and Rhonda worked very hard in the yard. Gardens were weeded. The grass was cut. The sidewalk's were edged and washed clean with the hose. Rhonda's Dad would say with a big smile, "Honey, people stop and take pictures it looks so good." Daddy had many more where that one came from.

Rhonda enjoyed seeing her Daddy with a smile and showing him she could work as hard as a four year old could. There was a method to her madness. If her Daddy could not get the lawn mower started in about six pulls, he would say, "Come on Rhonda, we are going to the store." Rhonda knew exactly which store it was and what they had to offer. Rhonda would sit on her Daddy's lap and steer the car. She felt so confident and secure with her Dad, it was noticed by all with her big smile and a head held high. Entering the store, there were tires of all sizes. There were also lawn mowers of all sizes and most of all, bicycles of all sizes. Rhonda's eyes were like big olives. She looked as though she was looking into the eyes of Santa Clause. Rhonda was very patient. She did receive two bicycles from that store just because the lawn mower did not start. She received one bike at a time, of course.

CHAPTER 3

Rhonda was getting ready to start the first grade. Nannie worked extra hard on the dresses Rhonda would have for the season. The bus did not come to the house to pick her up, Rhonda walked to school. It was a good mile and a half. On rainy days, someone would take her to school. Rhonda's big accomplishments in first grade were penmanship and drawing whatever the teacher, Mrs. Birdglass, had requested. Mrs. Birdglass said to Rhonda, "Your rainbow was the prettiest of all." This comment was the only one she had ever given Rhonda, except to make a remark about the lunch bag that had fallen out of Rhonda's locker. After looking inside and seeing only half of sandwich, a piece of fruit for lunch, she asked the class, "Who eats like a bird?" Rhonda waited until most of the class was out of the room to go to lunch before retrieving her bird-like lunch. What Mrs. Birdglass did not know was Rhonda's Nannie had a frozen chocolate shake in the freezer for her every day when she arrived home from school.

One evening at the latter part of first grade Mother was not home from work. When asked, the reply was, "She will be here shortly." Mother arrived home and Rhonda came out of her room and saw a big white bandage on her Mother's shin. Rhonda, in a soft voice, asked, "Are you going to be alright?" Rhonda's Mother replied, "Yes Rhonda, I am going to be fine." Rhonda noticed when it was time to eat her Mother would take a handful of pills, all at one time before she ate.

Rhonda did not question any of the strange things she saw. Rhonda also noticed her Mother was not home like before, she was in the hospital and the whole family would go see her. Rhonda thought this was a special treat because there was a big bin outside of the elevators filled with children's tennis shoes. Rhonda would change her shoes then everyone could go to Mother's room. Rhonda asked one day, "Why do I have to change shoes?" Her Nannie explained that tennis shoes were soft soles and would not make noise like hard sole shoes. The soft shoes keep footsteps of little ones quiet for the patients in the hospital.

Rhonda's birthday was about to roll around and she was so excited. She had invited some of her classmates and friends she played with in the neighborhood. Rhonda's Mother was home and this too made Rhonda happy. Her Mother asked her Father if he would go and get more ice cream? Daddy asked if Rhonda would like to go and steer the car? Of course this answer was a big "Yes". When Rhonda and her Daddy returned home, they saw a truck with a trailer on the side yard of their house. Rhonda's Daddy went towards the truck and a man started talking with him. Rhonda was called over and to her surprise she saw what was inside of the trailer: a beautiful brown, black and white pony. Rhonda immediately said, "His name is Fury." All the kids perked up and lined up to ride. Fury was not the only gift; there was the blanket, saddle, and all hard ware to ride. Needless to say, everyone was there until dark riding Fury.

Rhonda waited for her Daddy to get home from work. Daddy arrived and saddled up Fury. Daddy took the reins and held them while she mounted Fury. Daddy, with the reins still in his hand, walked along side while Rhonda rode. Unfortunately it had rained that morning and there were puddles of mud on the side of the road. Daddy slipped and went down fast. Fury took off with Rhonda on his back. Daddy gave a loud yell, "Take hold of the reins and pull back hard and say Woe." Rhonda grabbed the reins and pulled back and did exactly what her Daddy said. Fury kept running as fast as he could. Suddenly Rhonda heard a loud whistle. Fury must have heard it too because his feet started skidding on the rocks. He stopped in his tracks. Rhonda had the reins in her hand and she pulled to the left and said, "Getty up." Fury turned around and started slowly back home. When they got home, surprisingly, Fury trotted up to my Mother, who had whistled, and stopped right in front of her. Rhonda got down and said, "That was enough for one day." Mother took Fury back to his shelter and when she came back in the house Rhonda noticed her dress was torn. Rhonda asked her about it and she replied, "Fury bit me on my thigh." "What did you do?" My sister asked. Mother said very lady-like, "I doubled up my fist and hit him in the neck." Despite Mother's blows of correction, Fury would bite Mother every time she went out to feed him. Fury became too mean and we had to give him back. Mother did in fact knock Fury on his butt and quietly spoke these words. "That's all I need, is someone to call animal control and say I am committing cruelty to a pony." Mr. Intringer took Fury back and he shot him. Fury kicked his son in the side and punctured a lung. This certainly called for drastic measure. I thanked Mr. Intringer and told him I was sorry to here about his son, who was recovering, but I did understand why this had to be done. I am glad and thankful Fury did not harm any of the children who were at the birthday party.

Mother was in the hospital a lot now. When she was home, Rhonda would have to be careful of the David jar that had a drain hose connected in the lid, leading from her stomach. Rhonda can still remember her black velvet robe with white satin around the cuffs and her pockets were lined with it too. She always had a smile and was very interested in what Rhonda learned that day. Rhonda depended on her Nannie for comfort because she could not sit on Mothers lap nor could she give Mother a hug. The whole family thought Rhonda would knock over that jar with the hose in it. Rhonda really did understand it was connected to Mother.

In the mornings, Douglas, Betty and Rhonda would dress for school, eat and leave in the car. Rhonda remembers the ambulance sitting in front of the house ready to take Mother back to the hospital. Rhonda was now nine years of age and in the third grade. Although Rhonda was growing up fast due to the age difference in her siblings, she was still a little girl who needed direction. Sometimes it felt as though all of the parenting went towards her older brother and sisters, and Rhonda was to follow their lead in life. Rhonda was loved by all of her family members but both her parents were virtually absent. Rhonda's Father worked out of town Monday through Friday and her Mother worked and was now dying of cancer.

Rhonda's Nannie was both Mother and Father to Rhonda. Nannie handled the discipline, she was the one Rhonda ran to when the lightening struck and thunder roared. Nannie and Rhonda talked about her Mother's illness. Nannie told Rhonda to remember what she learned in Church, regarding Heaven, Angles and all of Mothers pain and suffering would go away. Nannie also told Rhonda that when the time came to attend the wake not to cry. Crying was to be done inside the house not in public.

Rhonda woke on October 24, 1963 and got ready for school just like every other day. School started and after about an hour the teacher called her to the front of the class. She softly told Rhonda to get her things together she was going home. Rhonda's sister, Betty was waiting outside the classroom. Betty did not mention why they were going home and Rhonda had a sick feeling she already knew. They met Douglas, their brother, in the parking lot and he drove home. Rhonda walked in and saw her Uncle, his wife and many other people she did not know. Betty took her in there bedroom and told Rhonda her Mother had passed away. They both cried and hugged one another. They stayed in the bedroom for a long time talking. Rhonda did not want to go out the door with all the people she did not know. Rhonda asked Betty what was going to happen? Betty could not answer her question. Nannie could not answer that question and this worried Rhonda. Next thing Rhonda remembered was being in a strange long black car going to see her Mother's body. Rhonda was told her Mother was in Heaven and the body is just a shell, which held her Mother's soul.

The funeral home was a big red brick building with white pillars in front. The long black car pulled up to the front doors and they were let out and the big white doors opened. Rhonda was scared and did not know what to expect. She held on to her brother's hand very tightly. Inside the funeral home, was filled with different rooms and staircases leading up to more rooms. Rhonda and her brother entered and went to the left. The room was filled with flowers of all types. The smell of roses was most pungent. The sweetness was thick in the air from all the flowers, almost sickening. Mothers casket was silver blue. The lining was silver satin. Mother was wearing a beautiful baby blue gown with orchids pinned to her gown. Orchids, purple orchids, were her favorite flower. Rhonda kept remembering what her Nannie said about crying in public. Rhonda tried very hard not to cry, but to no avail the tears streamed down her freckled cheeks. When Rhonda and her brother got up to the casket, Rhonda asked her brother why was Mother so thin? Then she asked him if she could touch her hand. Her Mother's hand was so cold and so hard Rhonda's tears were no longer hidden. She tried not to let Nannie or her Daddy catch her crying. Her brother told her they needed to sit down so the other people could view Mothers body. As they turned around the room was so full there was no place for Bubba and Rhonda to sit. Bubba told Rhonda to go find her cousins. There were three of them and Rhonda did not like them very much. Rhonda never said anything to any body but she did not like them. Rhonda found them running up and down the staircase. She went and found somewhere to sit away from the smell of flowers. This was impossible. Finally Rhonda found a room upstairs with no one in it. She went in and discovered trays of sandwiches, trays of vegetables with dip and trays with chips and dips. Most of all there was a couch and chairs and no people. Rhonda stayed in this room for a long time and then one of her cousins walked in and told her, she was suppose to go back in the room with the family. Rhonda thought this night would never end. She just wanted to be alone.

Rhonda did not attend school for quite a while. Rhonda's family drove to Texas from Louisiana and stopped in two separate cities where the wake was held all over in each town. Rhonda did not attend the last two wakes nor did she attend the funeral. She was left with family members she had just met. Rhonda was not aware that her

Nannie was going to move into a trailer in her son's back yard. This devastated Rhonda. Finally they were back home. Rhonda did not pass the third grade due to all of her absence.

Rhonda's Father made the hardest decision in his life; he drove Rhonda to Pasadena, Texas to live with her Nannie.

The drive was long and hard for both of them. Rhonda was very close to her Father and he worshiped Rhonda. He did make a promise to Rhonda. Her Father told her he would pick her up in (1) one year. Rhonda was glad to see her Nannie but at the same time she now was losing her Father for one whole year and this seemed like an eternity.

Herein lies the beginning structure of PTSD, moving, losing Aunt Louise and Uncle Eddie even her dog, the loss of her Mother at such a young age. Losing the closest thing she knew as a parent, her Dad, who took her to live with the Nannie.

During this year, Rhonda took care of her Nannie as well as she could. Her Nannie had type one diabetes. Nannie would give herself an injection every morning and she put in one contact in her left eye. The contact would float around in her eye and it was up to Rhonda to find it and put it in the correct spot so Nannie could see. Rhonda was very gentle but still had the felling she was going to hurt her Nannie in some way.

Rhonda attended third grade again, in the following year. Rhonda did very well. Nannie babysat for extra money and Rhonda would go with her. Every Sunday, Rhonda and Nannie would go to church and they would watch the nursery. This is when Rhonda would get to help. It was not very often Rhonda saw her Uncle and Aunt or her cousins. This, of course, was Rhonda's choice. Nannie and Rhonda would go to supper every now and then but not as often as you would expect. Rhonda learned how to play canasta with Nannie. Rhonda could hardly hold all the cards in her little hands; they played with two decks of cards. On Sunday afternoon, Nannie would make a treat for the two of them. Skillet cornbread in buttermilk. At first it was a challenge but after a while Rhonda looked forward to it.

During the middle of the school year, Rhonda sprained her ankle. Rhonda had done this before but this one was bad. It was three times the size of a normal ankle and purple as an eggplant. Rhonda got to stay home with Nannie and lay on the couch and watch TV with Nannie all week. Rhonda's Father would call from time to time and still repeated his promise.

Rhonda and Nannie did not have air condition in the trailer. Fans were in all three rooms of the trailer. Rhonda would watch her Nannie cooking and she would sweat every time. When the weather was cooler Nannie would make a strawberry pie.

Rhonda could have eaten every bite of that pie. Big juicy strawberries in Nannies' special sauce and a piecrust that was so flaky the fan would separate the layers. Nannie would not give her recipes away to anyone. The year was almost over and as excited as Rhonda was so was she sad to leave her Nannie. Rhonda begged her Nannie to come home with her but to no avail. Rhonda understood she was receiving money from her Mother's death but had never ask why, how or who kept it.

Rhonda's Father called and gave Nannie the news that he would be there on Friday to pick Rhonda up. Rhonda was so excited. Her heart was beating so fast and the grin was from one ear to the other. Rhonda gave Nannie so many hugs that day, more than ever. Rhonda would go outside and sit on the metal stairs outside of the trailer and call Tiny. Tiny was an English bulldog that belonged to Nannie. Tiny and Rhonda were buddies from the start. Tiny would be waiting in the same spot every day when Rhonda got home from school. Tiny made the stay with Nannie much more fun and relaxing. Rhonda played with Tiny more than she had with her cousin's. The time came for Rhonda to go back to New Orleans with her Father. Rhonda took her Father outside and asked him if it was possible for her, Rhonda, to buy Nannie an air conditioner and a rug for the trailer. "It would make Nannie so much more comfortable, Daddy, please." Rhonda's Father told her yes and the next day an air conditioner and a rug came in a big truck. Rhonda took Nannie for a walk and made it a big surprise for Nannie when they returned home. Sure enough, Nannie was so surprised she cried. Rhonda held on to her waist and said, "Don't cry Nannie.

Now you won't be hot in the summer and you won't have to worry about your feet with the new rug on the floor." Nannie hugged Rhonda like never before and she hugged her right back. Nannie and Rhonda's Father was the love and stability in Rhonda's life at this point.

Living with her Nannie was probably the first normalcy in Rhonda's life. She was loved, guided, and a foundation was being laid down for a healthy ten-year-old. All these standards of morality were soon to be compromised.

Rhonda was now home and had her own room. Rhonda's brother, Douglas and sister, Betty still lived in the house as well. Everyone had their assigned chores everyday. The one thing Rhonda did not like was breakfast. Douglas would make eggs and toast for breakfast and Rhonda would sit at the table sometimes until lunch and was still looking at eggs. Douglas was told not to let Rhonda get up until she ate everything on her plate. Many a day there would be a stand off between Rhonda, her egg's and Douglas. There was a day when Douglas was cutting the grass and Rhonda's bike was on the front sidewalk. Douglas came inside and told Rhonda to pick her bike up and put it away.

Rhonda went outside and grabbed her bike by the handlebars, turned it very hard and quick right into the muscle of her right arm. When she removed it the muscle came out but no blood. Rhonda screamed and ran inside and Douglas followed. He laid Rhonda on the bed and told her to stay there. Douglas call Daddy and he came home and took Rhonda to the doctor's office. The doctor stitched it and Rhonda and her Father went home. Rhonda did not have to eat those eggs that day. This was also the first stitches Rhonda had. Rhonda made her rounds in the neighborhood and showed everybody who would give her the time of day.

The family was doing as good as to be expected until Douglas and Betty both wanted to leave the house. Rhonda was to go with one or the other because she was not to be left alone yet. Rhonda's Father could not take the arguing anymore and did the dumbest thing, Rhonda thought, in the world. Rhonda's Father married. This was not only a shock to the family but a disaster. Her name was Shirley. Shirley was a very large woman and so was her Mother. Betty refused to go to the grocery store because Shirley would come out with five grocery carts full of food. This was not because we were picky or big eaters, we were not, it was so she and her mother could eat all day. Shirley would eat a half-gallon of chocolate ice cream for breakfast ever day. For some unforeseen reason, Shirley was obsessed with the number of times Rhonda had a bowel movement in a week's time. She would ask her everyday, "Did you have a bowel movement today?" If Rhonda would say no, she was given a laxative. This laxative was white, thick and it tasted bad. If Rhonda threw it up, Rhonda had to clean it up. If Rhonda refused to clean it she was whipped with the laundry stick. Rhonda disliked her stepmother and the laxative and since dislike is being mentioned Rhonda did not think to highly of her stepmother's mother. Rhonda called home from school one day because she started her period for the first time. Shirley's mother was at the house and said in the background, "Bring her home, we'll give her castor oil. She won't call home again from school." What a <u>B#@(&</u>. Needless to say, this marriage did not last but one year. Rhonda's Father was told an ear full by her brother and sister and her Fathers best friend, Papa J who asked Rhonda, "Why do your legs look like a purple zebra?" Rhonda's Father set up residence in another state and was divorced in no time.

This was a time of destruction and deceit by everyone except Rhonda's Dad and Papa Jay. Douglas and Betty taught Rhonda to be sneaky and scheming at this was a very impressionable age, eleven. Discipline and a lot of anger and rage was added to Rhonda's PTSD. Resentfulness began to set in for everyone who was close to her. This would not have happen if there had been adult supervision and guidance which was lacking since Nannie moved out. Rhonda was on the edge of being out-of-control. The only guidance Rhonda had at this point was her older brother and sister, and they were in their early twenties and they thought it was funny to see their 12-year-old sister tipsy and staggering. Other times they did not have the time to take her, or watch her at home when asked by their Father.

Counseling was definitely needed at this point in life. Rhonda desperately needed an Earth's Hidden Angel.

CHAPTER 4

As the days, months and years passed after Rhonda's mother's death, the thoughts of the long and drawn out wakes, relatives she met and will never see again was still unresolved in Rhonda's mind. The stepmother from hell, failing the third grade, a glimmer of light was appearing in this tunnel. The light even had a name, May Lynn, Rhonda's soon to be new step mom. This particular light became brighter each day and it could not have come at a better time, it was 1967. Rhonda's Dad was gleaming with happiness. This was, as you well know by now, the most important factor to Rhonda. Rhonda's stay with Nannie taught her early of responsibilities, values, and most of all Love to hewn each quality of virtue to a sharp edge.

Rhonda now learned standards. There were boundaries, house rules, and a lot of respect.

Rhonda now in early teens, was a handful, with boys, smoking, and Rhonda, by now had a lot of emotional problems that were pushed inside and were never noticed let alone dealt with. She had hostility built up and here comes Lily, Mom's daughter. She showed Rhonda exactly what manipulation, lying and phoniness would get you... nowhere but flat on your back after a good–ole fist smacking and butt kicking. Rhonda had changed very quickly for the better.

It took a while for everyone, Mom, Dad, Lily and Rhonda to all fall into their respectful places and to quote Rhonda's Dad, "It was peace and harmony." Until the next problem popped up. Lily was a year older than Rhonda and the two got along pretty well. It felt like a family for the first time.

Lily and Rhonda would double date and come home to share secrets only known to them over a bowl of macaroni and cheese with chunks of ham and a good late night movie.

Lily and Rhonda were rewarded for their hard work by surprise weekend trips to Dolphin Island, Florida. Dad would get two rooms, one for he and mom and one for Lily and Rhonda.

Boys came and went so fast Dad would nick name all of them because he could not keep up with their names.

High school came and it was a new ball game. In New Orleans, the High Schools were not co-ed. The boy's high school was in one direction and the girls in the opposite.

The phone rang and Mom answered. The call informed us Nannie had passed away, needless to say this was very upsetting for all. Nannie's heart gave out. She had scraped her foot on the metal stairs out side her trailer door. Due to the diabetes, she developed gangrene. Nannie's heart was not strong enough to stand an operation that would take her leg up to the knee and the doctor suggested to wait it out. This was not easy for Rhonda, but yet another collection for her shelf of woe.

May Lynn saw right through a troubled Rhonda. May Lynn did what she could and she gave it her best shot. She made the woman that Rhonda is today. Rhonda was now promiscuous and had no clue who she was or was suppose to be. The years to come did not help Rhonda's situation at all, as a matter of fact it was the straw that broke the camels back to quote a phrase. Rhonda was truly lost now and the PTSD was in full bloom. Rhonda was now 17 years old.

Soon it was time for Lily to graduate. Rhonda had one more year and was not doing well in school. Lily and Mom had a very bad argument and Lily went to Rhonda's room and asked if she wanted to move out. Rhonda was shocked but concerned. Lily never fought with Mom in this manner. Lily and Rhonda left the house and found an apartment, if you could call it that. The front door did not work, therefore, you had to walk through the vacant apartment next door and jump onto the roof to the left. The apartment was on the second floor of a house. The neighborhood was less than desirable with drunks in and out of the Mom and Pop store on the corner. There were no lights on the streets and derelicts all around. Still they got the apartment. Rhonda tried to work as a bartender and go to school during the day. This lasted two months. Rhonda dropped out of high school with only three months to go until she would have graduated. Lily and Rhonda saved enough money to move in a more suitable neighborhood and managed to get a roommate to join in on the fun. When Lily and Rhonda were living together their method of getting food was not so conventional. It had gotten to the point when they would go out to eat both of them brought big purses' with them. This one Spanish restaurant would have 'all you could eat specials' and boy was it special. After taking a bite here and there, they would empty their plate into plastic containers in their big purse. Lily and Rhonda would have enough food for the next three weeks. Yes Rhonda would say they were lower than broke before moving in with their boyfriends. It was right after that they found boyfriends from different backyards and went their own ways.

Rhonda was in the kitchen of her new house and a knock came from the living room door. Rhonda looked out side and saw a white uniform with black trim around the cuffs and long collar. It was a sailor, an old friend of Rhonda's boyfriend. The gentleman said he was an old friend of Jake's and was in on leave, could he please wait inside for him? Yes he was more than welcome, Rhonda could not resist a man in a uniform and did he fill it in the right places. His name was Tate. Rhonda moved back with her parents and it was not long until she was pregnant. Tate was stationed in Maryland and lived in a trailer with his friend who traveled quite a bit. Rhonda flew to Maryland, via Washington D.C. and joined Tate. It was there they planned their wedding. Rhonda and Tate lived in a doublewide trailer. Tate's friend was traveling extensively and asked that the newlyweds watch over the trailer while he was gone. This worked out wonderfully until one morning Tate and Rhonda had just woke up and Rhonda went to the restroom. The next thing Tate heard was a crying scream, he ran into the bathroom and Rhonda's hands were full of blood. Tate was white as the Navy uniform he looked so handsome in. Rhonda asked for a towel and a hand getting up off the toilet. She explained to Tate, she thought she had to pee. Rhonda then saw Tate was not doing so well and instructed Tate to get the car warmed up and to please bring her clothes. "We need to go to the hospital on base." Upon arriving, no one was there at the point we were instructed to go. A nurse finally walked by and said, "The Doctor will see you now Rhonda." Rhonda was in a very cold room with one examining table, a long counter with a sink and metal cabinets above the counter. The Doctor came in and he did not say a word. As the doctor was examining Rhonda, the Doctor said, "Why are you crying? You are not pregnant and never were. I have women come in here and lose babies. You had an episode with your ovaries. The ovaries were suppressed. They, your ovaries, quit working for four months." Rhonda was in shock! Rhonda stated, "Two doctor's of gynecology said I was pregnant." "How can this be?" Rhonda asked with tears flowing. "The two (2) doctor's did a blood test and a urine test, plus a pelvic exam. I do not understand." The doctor then spoke up and said without hesitation, "Get up, clean yourself and the table. I will get the nurse to bring in your husband." Shaking like a leaf in a hurricane, Rhonda did what the doctor asked of her. Tate walks in with a bewilder look and said, "You B!^@$." Rhonda looked at the doctor and asked him, "What did you tell my husband?" "That you were not pregnant and never were." The doctor began to sympathize with Tate as if Rhonda had tricked him. Rhonda interrupted, "Tate, I was diagnosed by not one but two doctors' in New Orleans that I was pregnant. I would not do such a vicious act to you. Please believe me." Rhonda was still in tears knowing she lost a baby and was on the verge of a divorce in the same day. Tate finally believed Rhonda after speaking with the doctors' in New Orleans, which Rhonda insisted on calling. From that day on, Rhonda was very Lilyry of this Asian gynecologist. This in its self was not Rhonda. Rhonda did not have a bigoted bone in her body. It was very clear that she was upset with this doctor and would be for a long time.

Tate and Rhonda did come to the realization that they had lost a child. Rhonda's Dad had nicknamed the baby Roscoe. Rhonda would go to the laundromat once a week. New faces made new acquaintances and conversation. Rhonda would make it a habit to call her older sister, Bobbie, who was now in her late 30's. Bobbie lived in San Antonio with her husband number 4 and her son, Roy. Bobbie was packing a box of old clothes and items from around the house she thought Rhonda might enjoy. Bobbie was a drinking alcoholic, which Rhonda was unaware because of their age difference. Bobbie was 17 years older than Rhonda. Rhonda waited for the package to come but it never did and there was no answer when Rhonda would call Bobbie. Tate came home early one day and I knew something was terribly wrong. Tate asked me to follow him to the bedroom. He sat me on the bed and he sat close to me holding my hands. "Rhonda," Tate said, "Your Dad called the base today and the call was routed to my superior officer. I have bad news for you. Bobbie is dying and you have a plane ticket waiting for you at the Washington D.C. airport." Rhonda went numb. As the tears ran down her freckled face, Rhonda asked when she had to leave and if Tate was going to join her. Tate exclaimed, "No, I can't go now on short notice. Your ticket is waiting for you now. Your Dad will met you in San Antonio and will take you straight to Fort Sam Hospital where your family is waiting for you." Rhonda, dazed and oh so confused, packed a bag quickly for the two hour ride to Washington D.C. Tate and Rhonda embraced and both said together, "I love you!" Rhonda entered the plane and was brought a drink immediately. The flight attendant said all had been pre-arranged by your Dad. Rhonda was brought several drinks and before she knew it the plane was landing in San Antonio.

Rhonda was so glad to see her Dad but the situation was all to intense to realize the length of time in which she last saw her Dad. The car ride was over before she knew it. Rhonda's Dad held her hand as they entered a red brick building. Dad had walked us to a little room where family members and relatives were waiting for us. Dad announced to the family he and I would go and say our good-by's to Bobbie and would everyone please wait until we were back before they left the hospital. Daddy and Rhonda walked down a long corridor and turned right into a ward. There was patience on the right and left side of the room all in a row. Daddy had pasted Bobbie's bed. He did not recognize her. Bobbie had deep auburn hair and it was now snow white. Rhonda called to her Dad in a low voice and he turned around and Rhonda pointed to the bed Bobbie was in. Bobbie was hooked up to every machine possible and Daddy and Rhonda both only heard the heart monitor. It was so hard for Daddy to hold back his tears. Daddy and I said a silent prayer and kissed her on her fore head. Daddy and Rhonda had just walked out of the door of the ward and we heard the long beeeeeeep of the heart monitor. Bobbie's heart had stopped as if she was waiting for us to see her once more before joining the Lord, Mother and Nannie.

When that sound met Rhonda's ears', her legs buckled and she almost fell in the corridor. Daddy and an attendant caught her just before Rhonda hit the floor. Rhonda was given a cold compress for her head and a drink of water. It only took a short while before Rhonda was back to normal.

Rhonda was told that Bobbie only had one-fourth of her stomach, and half of her intestines and the cause of death was cirrhosis of the liver. Rhonda had no idea her sisters situation was so bad. To this day, she wished somebody had told her.

Tate and Rhonda moved back to New Orleans when Tate's tour was up. They lived with his parents for a while until they could afford a place of their own. Tate's family always kept their distance from Rhonda and was on the verge of being cold. Tate's Father had nothing to do with Rhonda. He viewed Rhonda as "trapping Tate into a marriage." Possibly because he was to damn cold to fell anything.

Rhonda did make a break through with Tate's sister, Tilly. Tilly's youngest girl had cystic fibrosis and Rhonda's heart went out to her. She was so tiny and frail Rhonda thought even holding her was a scary event. As you can tell Rhonda did not scare easily. It was about the third week back in town and Rhonda found a town house that was perfect. It was close to Tate's work, price was right, renting of course and not far from each of their parents. It was not complete until they purchased a puppy. Felicia, a miniature schnauzer. Tate's family had 2 or 3. Felicia was silver and cute as a bug.

She liked every body and every body liked her.

Tate and Rhonda were getting along all right. It was nothing to write home about, it was going to take effort on both parts they were going to make it as a couple. Tate and Rhonda used nothing for avoiding getting pregnant. It was never discussed. The marriage was about one and a half years now. Rhonda landed a good position as a personal secretary to the president of a film company and Tate went into the oil business. They expected the 1970's to be a good one.

Not very often did Rhonda miss a day's work, but this particular morning she was not feeling well at all. Rhonda was running a temperature, felt weak and very tired. Tate's last words to her were, "You better go to work." Tate also added "I'll call later on." Tate went off to work. Tate was gone about one hour and there was a loud banging on the front door.

Rhonda got up and put her jeans on and a sweater that was lying on the floor from the night before. She walked down the stairs to the front door and unlocked everything but the chain. Rhonda opened the door and peaked out of the 2-inch gap and saw a big black man. Rhonda asked," Can I help you?" The man replied, "Is Tate home?" Rhonda said, "Tate went to work and can be back in 5 minutes or 5 hours." "Can I tell him you stopped by?" The man looked at me with a stare and said, "No". "I was suppose to meet him here at 8:00 a.m." As the man said the time he also looked down at his watch.

Rhonda noticed he was dirty. His clothes had an unclean look about them. Rhonda closed the door and went back upstairs to go to bed. Rhonda lay there for about 5 minutes and this time the knock was harder than before. Rhonda put her clothes on again and went down stairs. It was the same man. Rhonda did as before and did not unchain the lock. Rhonda asked, "It's you again. What can I do for you?" The man replied. "My brother dropped me off and I don't have a ride. May I use your phone to call him?" Rhonda thought for a moment and said, "Yes. Come in." Rhonda left the front door completely open and told the man the phone was just around the wall. Rhonda was trying to think of how did he know Tate? Rhonda really did not know everything Tate was involved in so that was my justification. Rhonda was trying to light a cigarette and had her head down looking at the lighter. Then she felt a hard thud on the left side of her head. She looked up in amazement and saw it was a gun and said, "Please don't hurt me. Do you want silver, something to eat, money?" He heard, "Money" "Go get it" Where is it?"

At this point Rhonda was not thinking clearly and at the same time she was trying to remember what she was suppose to do in a situation like this. "Upstairs," Rhonda replied. Not trying to be funny at all I said, "It's upstairs in my purse, wait here and I'll get it for you." Rhonda will never forget the deep laugh she got from that one. He said, "I'll go with you so you don't do anything funny." As we were walking up the stairs Rhonda knew if he saw the unmade bed he was going to rape me. We entered the room and he forgot all about the money. He insisted Rhonda sat on the edge of the bed. Rhonda did as he asked. Then he started taking off her pants and underwear. He told Rhonda if she made a sound or if Tate was to come home, he would blow her fucking brains all over the wall and he would kill Tate too. Rhonda did not make a sound. Rhonda was not thinking of what he was doing, Rhonda was praying to the good Lord to please let me live through this and kept Tate away. The rapist was performing oral sex with her and then he raped her. Rhonda did talk him into putting the gun on the floor beside the bed so he would not forget and shoot her in his moment of invasion. This was key to the police to locate what area he was from. Luckily he did put the gun down and it was over quickly. Rhonda got up and started to dress and remembered, "Give him something that is identifiable." The paper envelope that her check came in was very unusual and she tore off a piece and gave him her phone number. Rhonda was talking about everything and any thing at this point. Rhonda just wanted him and his 35 revolver gone. Rhonda walked in front of him down the stairs and opened the door for him to leave. He turned to her and said, "If you tell anyone I was here, I will come back and kill you." It sounded, pretty sincere to me. Rhonda told him she would keep it a secret and she was looking forward to the phone call. He was out the door. RHONDA WAS ALIVE. SHE MADE IT. Rhonda ran to the kitchen and called Tate at work. She spoke with his boss and she never said what happened, but he could tell something was drastically wrong. He told Rhonda Tate would be there within 10 minutes. Rhonda said thank you and hung up. Rhonda then got a chair from the dinning table and pushed it under the doorknob of the front door. Rhonda barricaded the back door. She ran upstairs and showered 3 times and then got in again and showered more. She felt so dirty. He reaked of alcohol. Tate was now home and had not a clue why he could not get in the front door. Rhonda kept on asking is that really you? Tate at this point got very irritated. Rhonda pulled every thing away from the door and let him in and told him what had happened. Rhonda was expecting, oh maybe, a little concern but she was pushed to the side and Tate called his parents. Of all the people? Why? He finally asked, "Are you alright?" "Hell no." Rhonda replied. Rhonda felt as though all the nasty dirty filthy scum in the world just invaded my most private world; her body and soul. She was scared to death. When you have a revolver pointed at your temple you tend to hear, "If you tell anyone I will come back and kill you."

Rhonda did not receive a hug nor affection, Tate asked, "Did you enjoy it?" As if she had planned this horrible thing. Rhonda did not say much any more to him. He instructed Rhonda to get into the car. They were off to his parent's house. Rhonda was not even allowed to call her parents, who lived only four blocks away.

Tate and Rhonda arrived at his parent's house and Rhonda went to the kitchen and sat at the bar. His mother was in the kitchen and she asked if Rhonda was all right. My answer was the same. "No!"

Tate's Dad walked into the kitchen holding his black socks and said harshly, "Why did you open the door?" Rhonda replied, "The person asked for Tate not once but twice, I thought he knew him." Tate's Dad said, "Thought that was your problem, you are to blame for opening the fucking door." "This would have never happened if you would not have opened the door." He concluded, "I am late for work."

It was at this point Rhonda went numb. What Rhonda did not know was this was the PTSD. At twenty-one Rhonda was sometimes a lonely child and other times a grown woman. The time to find a Hidden Angel was now. To no avail she pushed on.

There were at least fifteen police and ten plainclothes men inside the house. They were gathered at the dinning room table. The Chief of Police was there and he was instructing each of their duties for this case. Two undercover policemen were assigned to Rhonda and they were not to leave her side at any time. Rhonda started looking for Tate. He was nowhere to be found. Rhonda asked his sister if she had seen him and she said, "Right after he dropped you off he went to his best buddies house." No message, see you later, or nothing. This told Rhonda a lot and with the comment before Rhonda knew where her marriage was headed. Rhonda could only deal with one thing at a time. Her mind was so confused; it all seemed like a horrible dream. The two detective's assigned to her came to Rhonda and said, "Rhonda, we must leave now." She went with them. As they drove off and Rhonda asked, "Where are we going?" Charles said in a soft voice, "We will make a routine stop at the hospital to get you examined and then we will go downtown to the station to take your deposition." This particular detective was very nice and Rhonda attached to him like white on rice. Rhonda asked if he would stay with me and please do not leave me alone. He did just that. This man never left her side. He even went to the bathroom with her. He stood by the sinks but she knew he was there. Rhonda had to give them a blow by blow of every thing that happened several times and then she looked at pictures. The only question from Rhonda was, "How did he, the rapist, know Tate's name?" Charles looked at me and said, "Rhonda, he read it from your mail box outside." Before she knew it, it was 10:00p.m. The first face Rhonda saw was her big brother and was that the most comforting sight she had ever seen. Tate walked in a little after. Douglas asked the detectives if there was any more questions for his little sister, he wanted to bring her home. The detective's said "No, and if there is anything else we can call her." "It's been a long day." Rhonda replied, she thanked them and Doug took her by her arm and led her out to his car.

Doug and Tate, who said not two words to Rhonda, sped away. Rhonda had not a clue where they were going nor did she care. Rhonda's mind was drifting with everything that had happened to her. She felt as though every one was out to do her harm. Did she leave anything out that would help her case? This feeling was with Rhonda for quite some time. Next thing Rhonda knew Doug was opening her door and helping her out of the back seat. Rhonda did not recognize the building all she knew was she was safe by her brother's side. Tate was there and that was it. His comment, "Did you enjoy it?" hit Rhonda like a ton of bricks.

Rhonda, Douglas and Tate entered two wide doors then we were asked, "A table for three?" Douglas said in a deep voice, "We would prefer a booth towards the back, please." The waiter waved his arm toward the back of the restaurant and said, "This way please." We followed the waiter and as Rhonda looked around she noticed the place was huge and not a lot of people were there. There were lots of tables in the middle and booths lined both sides of the restaurant. Our booth was just as Douglas asked for. Before the waiter could say a word, Douglas ordered for all of us. Martini's all a round and please keep them coming for my sister. The waiter said, "I will be right back." Before Rhonda knew it, she had drank nine Martini's and walked out of that place straight as a judge.

On the ride home the only words Rhonda heard was, "I can't believe she drank nine Martini's and she looks and sounds like she did not have one." They were back at the scene of the crime, Tate and Rhonda's townhouse. The police had been there to get as much evidence as possible and it showed. Things were moved around, the sheets were gone from the bed and the house had black powder all over everything. Rhonda was so tired she said she was going to bed. Douglas said, "I'll be there in a minute." Rhonda was relieved that Doug said that, because she did not want to sLilyp in the same bed with a man who would think let alone ask if she enjoyed any part of the most vulgar, nasty, haneous thing a woman could ever go through. Doug slept with Rhonda for two (2) weeks. Rhonda felt so afraid and withdrawn from everyone. Doug was there when Rhonda needed him now that she was older.

The paranoia was overwhelming at this point. Rhonda did not leave the apartment unless she was with someone she knew very well and she did not answer the door. Rhonda was told he would kill her if she said anything to anyone.

As the days passed, Rhonda tried to return to work. This was a disaster. Rhonda became so suspicious of anyone who approached her she would start to cry. Needless to say, Rhonda resigned. Now she was back at the place that it happened.

Rhonda had lost some weight but she thought it was due to the situation. Rhonda was not eating, she had lost her appetite and with everything else going on in her marriage she did not realize just how much she had lost. Rhonda finally got the nerve to go to her parent's house. This was another hard thing for Rhonda to face. Tate did not like Rhonda's step mom.

Rhonda's father took one look at her and asked if she was all right. That was like breaking the dam. Rhonda fell in front of her father's chair where he was sitting and just began to bawl like a baby. Rhonda's father and step mom all joined in on well deserved water works. After their good cry together, Rhonda's step mom asked if she had been eating, Rhonda said she did not have an appetite. Rhonda's step mom asked if she could be pregnant. Rhonda stopped and said, "No, No, I can't be."

As much as it hurt Rhonda to even think such a thing, she and her step mom went and got a pregnancy test. It was positive.

It could not have been Tate's, Rhonda had not slept with him since before the rape. Tate was treating her as if she were damaged goods. Rhonda was surprised they were still under the same roof. Rhonda's step mom was her savior during this time. Rhonda finally got on the scale and realized she was down 30 pounds in one month.

It was decided that Rhonda should have an abortion due to the stress of everything that had happened. Rhonda was in no shape mentally to raise a child of any color at this point in her life. It would always remind her of the rape. This was not how the good Lord intended for her to become a mother. Rhonda's step mom spoke to Tate and every one was in agreement. The appointment was set and Rhonda, Tate and step mom went to the clinic. Rhonda was taken back and the disrobing had begun. The nurse came in and asked if she could talk to Rhonda? Rhonda said, "Yes." The nurse was a very pretty black lady and she said "I am aware of your whole situation but I need to tell you the Doctor doing the procedure is black." Rhonda thought for a moment and said, "With all due respect, one got me into this one can get me out." This nurse looked at Rhonda and said, "I am so glad you have that attitude. You will be fine." She then rolled Rhonda out of the waiting area and into the procedure room. The first thing that happened was the Doctor came up to the bedside and told Rhonda, "Not to worry, you will be fine."

Rhonda was released with antibiotics and a caution slip stating, Watch For High Fever. Tate insisted he was going to take care of Rhonda. Rhonda was put to bed and given an antibiotic as soon as she arrived home. Rhonda later woke and asked if Tate would get her some soup. Tate was watching TV at the foot of their bed and said just a minute. The minute turned into 30 then 45 minutes.

Rhonda, with a fever of 102 degrees, dresses and drives to the corner store and gets 2 cans of soup. Everyone in the store asked if she was all right? Rhonda drove home with the soup and began to heat it in a pan and here comes Tate. I told you just to wait a minute. Rhonda did not even dignify that with a twitch. Rhonda took her soup and a drink upstairs and got back into bed. Rhonda brought her fever down and took the rest of the antibiotics. Things were not good at home and it started to show. Rhonda would go out during the day and look for a job and when she got home Tate was there with the twins Rhonda used to go to high school with and they lived just around the corner. Mary and Teresa would look at Rhonda and say "Hi" "How are you doing?" and Tate would ask Rhonda to make the girls a drink. They seem to be your guest Tate, you are capable to serve them yourself.

Rhonda now knew that the marriage was over, Tate did not even remake the bed that Rhonda made before she left to look for a job. This was very clear to Rhonda, and you, the reader, can draw your own opinion. Rhonda announced she was moving out and she would send for the furniture she wanted All the refinished furniture had to stay, Tate demanded it was his. During Tate's tour of duty with the navy, they lived up north and would find old furniture to refinish. This was Rhonda's hobby. The furniture was walnut and had lion heads for the foot of the chair's, one upright and one was a rocker. That was the only thing Rhonda was requesting to take with her. That was a big "No", "It's mine." At this point Rhonda said keep it all I don't want anything that reminds me of you or the town house. Before Rhonda left, there were a lot of empty jars in the cabinet. Rhonda took them outside in the adjoining field in the back of the town house. The only thing standing in this field was an old brick fireplace. Rhonda threw the jars against the bricks and with each one she got her anger out. Rhonda found that this was just a temporary fix. Rhonda moved in with her parents and proceeded with a divorce.

CHAPTER 5

Even after Rhonda was gone for two weeks, she received a call from Tate who was asking Rhonda to please come back. Rhonda's answer was always the same, "I think we learned a lot and matured from our ups and downs but we also knew it was not going to work." Tate was pretty persistent and even had Mary, one of the twins, call Rhonda and say, "Rhonda, you are all he talks about any more. Tate genuinely loves you." This did not influence Rhonda in the least. Rhonda continued with her plans of a divorce and landing a good job.

Rhonda's step-mom, May Lynn, gave her the name of an attorney, Mr. Littleton. Rhonda's Nannie had babysat with his children when she was living with Rhonda. Mr. Littleton was also a friend of Rhonda's father.

Rhonda made an appointment and Tate's calls continued to the point, May Lynn would tell him Rhonda was not home. The appointment date came around and Rhonda went. Mr. Littleton was extremely nice and this made Rhonda a little uncomfortable. As Rhonda was describing what the reasons were, Mr. Littleton got up from his chair and approached Rhonda in an unprofessional way. Mr. Littleton had put his arm around Rhonda and Rhonda lifted it off. Rhonda said "Mr. Littleton, I am seeking a divorce, can you conduct yourself in a professional way or not?" Mr. Littleton replied, "Rhonda, you have grown into such a lovely young woman, I just wanted to comfort you. Should I give you a call so we can go out for a drink?" Rhonda, gathered her purse and stood up and said, "I do not think that will ever be necessary?" Rhonda was going to try to forget this ever happened because she knew he was friends with her father. May Lynn knew immediately something was wrong when Rhonda returned home. Rhonda told her about the advances in Mr. Littleton's office. May Lynn said, "Your father must never hear of this Rhonda. Especially now, after your ordeal, I don't know what he will do." Rhonda's father did in fact find out and he went to see Mr. Littleton. The next thing we knew Mr. Littleton and his family's house was up for sale and they left New Orleans very quickly. Rhonda knew her father was an influential man she just did not know how influential he was until this happened.

Rhonda had a very good friend in New Orleans and she still does, Lena. Rhonda dated Lena's brother off and on but became friends, which is more that some can say after all this time. Lena recommended her attorney to Rhonda. The divorce was complete in one year. Napoleonic Law requires separation of a married couple for one year before a divorce can be granted. Rhonda was very unsure of herself and still very cautious to a fault. Every one of her friends knew why Rhonda was like this but it was strange behavior to those who did not know.

It was six months after the rape; Rhonda was sitting with her parents in their home eating supper. Rhonda busted out in tears and her father gave her this blank stare as to what can I do, May Lynn dropped her fork, Rhonda ask if she could use their telephone in their bedroom. May Lynn said, "Take as long as you need", "We'll check in on you later." Rhonda called the rape crisis hotline. Rhonda does not remember the lady's name she spoke with but bless her soul, she said what Rhonda needed to here at that moment and talked her through the process for two hours. This phone call made all the difference in the world to Rhonda. She was a new person as she opened her parents door, walked through the hall and into the den where her father looked at her with such loving eyes and May Lynn just stood up and hugged her so hard we were both out of breath. Rhonda turned to her father and it was apparent when there eyes met everything is going to be alright. Rhonda did seem to be more relaxed and started to see things more clearly now. Rhonda was at last, functional again.

Rhonda finally got a good job at a hospital, secretary for the Director of the Foundation. Rhonda expanded her knowledge and gained confidence and learned how to develop black and white film, more importantly she was learning the computer for the first time. Rhonda was designing the forms for data entry for new contributors and corrections sheets for existing clients. Rhonda was excited and enjoyed her job. She met people who later became her friends. Rhonda was on her 4th year of employment and the Director came up to her and asked, "Do you have any suggestions for building morale between departments?" Rhonda replied, "Not at this moment but I will brainstorm and get back with you." The Director said, "Good, we have 2 days before we go to the Board of Directors with it."

Rhonda began to think about bringing the different departments together and it hit her. In order to bring them together you must place them against each other in winning games. Rhonda started the bowling league in the winter and the volleyball league in the summer. It went on for some time after Rhonda left the hospital. The ironic thing about working at the hospital was Rhonda was born there. Rhonda then put together and organized the Lamaze classes. Rhonda was responsible for getting the teachers for the class and making weekly scheduling for the mothers and fathers to be. All meetings throughout the hospital went through Rhonda. Rhonda was growing and most of all learning, dealing with top contributors to the hospital. Rhonda was enjoying every aspect of her life and it showed.

Teams with captains were in order and scheduled were made. Dates and time coordinated with the different shifts and the games began. The meeting between the hospital managers was set and all was in order. It was time for Rhonda to go on vacation. She gave the duty of the Lamaze classes to the head nurse to distribute so classes would go on with out a hitch, and they did. It was very rewarding to have accomplished all this in a world that was growing so fast. Rhonda was very honored that the Directors gave her such a task to undertake. Rhonda's gratitude was overwhelming.

It was now time for a vacation, a two week vacation. Rhonda was excited to see Lily and her family. It took Rhonda eight hours to drive to San Antonio but it was pretty scenery and the anticipation of two weeks off made the trip even shorter. Rhonda finally arrived in SA. Knocked on Lily's door and we hugged and talked for hours just playing catch-up. We relaxed the first day and the second day Lily was making phone calls. Rhonda asked her what she was up to and she replied, "I am going to get you hooked up." Rhonda was surprised and it really did not cross her mind until Lily said something. Rhonda was very content with her life. Granted Rhonda had no life at this point so a little excitement was in store. Lily was planning a crap's party and a card game afterwards. We had good eats, plenty of beer and we were ready to go. Lily and Rhonda of course started early but this was o.k. The two of us were known for holding our liquor. People started to arrive and it was getting extra exciting knowing Rhonda had a blind date. Lily, most of the time knew Rhonda's taste, but Rhonda did not know if she was pulling my leg or on the level. Rhonda answered the door and it was the couple that brought her blind date. Technically he followed them in his truck so he could make a quick get away if he did not approve of what he saw. All of us had lots of fun, more than Rhonda had in a long time. David did not leave until 10:00 a.m. and did make sure to ask if he was invited back that evening. Rhonda said yes.

Rhonda and David spent the rest of her vacation together, talking, getting to know each others goals and plans for the future and the question arose, "Would you consider moving to San Antonio and living with me?" David asked. Rhonda waited a short while to answer this question and finally Rhonda said yes. David added, "If it works out good and if it does not work out, we can part as friends." Rhonda looked into David's sky blue eyes and said, "You have a deal."

Rhonda did have a secret dream she always thought of but never discussed it with anyone. Not even Lily. Rhonda wanted to live in the country and raise farm animals, and have children. She wanted to eat off the land, grow her own food and have a peaceful life.

Rhonda told Lily what she and David decided to do and Lily became excited. Both of them at the same time said "Let's call Mom." Rhonda got on the phone and told Mom, May Lynn, the news of her pending move. Rhonda explained there was something very right about this decision, she could feel it inside and reassured Mom everything was going to be all right.

The rest of the vacation was going by so fast and David was by Rhonda side the entire time she was there. This did make leaving very hard and it showed. David said he would call every night. David kept his word.

Rhonda gave her two-week notice at work and was very happy about her decision. It was time for a change and she had gotten a lot of experience working for the hospital for 5 years. For her diligence and excellent work habits, the Executor of the Hospital gave Rhonda an outstanding letter of recommendation. The two weeks were swiftly coming to an end and the hospital gave Rhonda a going away party. Rhonda was overwhelmed at all the people who attended. It seem as though every head of the different departments came by just to say good luck on her new adventure. Rhonda was very blessed and thankful for all of the well wishes.

All of Rhonda's things were packed and the boxes were ready for loading in the garage. David came the next day and had one day to rest and turn around and bring Rhonda and her things to their new home. Rhonda drove her car, which was filled, to the brim. David had brought his truck and everything fit like a glove. They arrived in San Antonio and were at David's house, a small white center block house with brown trim around each window and door. The porch was at least leaning towards the door to make visitors feel more welcome. Entering the front door was the living room, dining room and the kitchen all was open. The rest room was off to the left of the dinning room and lead to the first bedroom, which was separated by a closet to another small bedroom. It was perfect for a bachelor but needed a lot of help.

David was renting from a friend who lived just up the road from David and Rhonda. It was very reasonable priced. The house was situated in a valley with a hill on both sides. The foundation was shifting, cracking the walls and the windows sometimes shut and other times they did not. There was one air conditioning unit in the living room and Texas was hot in the summer and cold in the winter. Heat was a wood burning stove sitting in the middle of one side of the living room. This called for a lot of cuddling. David and Rhonda lived there very happily for one year and discovered they were going to have a baby. It was not planned but it sure was a pleasant surprise to both.

Rhonda had found a job not far from their house and she was doing well. Ironically it was a home for unwed mothers. Rhonda was the head of a small computer department, which consisted of only Rhonda. Rhonda had two bosses' that where both Methodist preachers. Rhonda had worked there for about one year before she became pregnant and she waited until the eighth month of her pregnancy to quit. David and Rhonda got married two months before the baby was born.

This was also the time when David's parents, Mr. and Mrs. Whittman, found a small house in the country and gave David the deal of a life time. David, being a carpenter, could fix the house up in the country and they would take it off of our payments to his grandmother, who paid cash for the house and sixteen acres. David and Rhonda owned half and his parents owned the other half. We moved, and Rhonda was almost nine months pregnant. The house was condemned, and the lavatory facility was not quite useable. David and a very large Rhonda had to use a five-gallon bucket until the correct pipes were hooked up to the sewer. This was their top priority. Next came the heat. The house was built in 1918 and there was no heat. There was propane, but all the jets were capped off. For the first year, David and Rhonda lived in the bedroom and kitchen, closing off the rest of the house because it was either too hot or too cold. Rhonda had thought that the process of fixing up the house was slow going because of the new baby. A beautiful baby girl named Rachel.

It wasn't until the move that Rhonda noticed a big change in David. David was coming home from work and the house did not bother him at all the way it was. Rhonda put a lot of trust in David and did not push the issue. It went on for along time. If his friends would stop by they would drink beer and work on the house or they would drink beer and drink more beer. The next adventure for David was a garden to grow vegetables. David would come home and drink beer but this time he had the tiller in the other hand and could not walk to the house to get another beer so Rhonda was on call not only for him.

Now he had a choice, to drink and work on the house, or to drink and play with the tiller in the garden. The worst was his drinking because he would drink all afternoon and night then eat and pass out. He did not even wake up to use the restroom he would wet the bed. Rhonda would have to wash the sheets every day and pull the mattress outside to dry. Rhonda knew David's one trait and she went straight for it. "If you continue to wet the bed I am going to buy a new mattress every six months." The bed-wetting stopped.

Rhonda held a lot inside her and no one really knew what was bothering her, but deep in side it was building ten times as fast as David was working on anything. At this point David decided that Rachel needed a brother or sister to play with. It was not long after the words were spoke that it happened. Rhonda would wash clothes, and hang them on the line. Rhonda was not to use the drier if the sun was out, even in the winter. Rhonda picked the vegetables from the garden, cleaned them, blanched them and sealed them for the freezer. The grocery list was checked and receipts were checked. Rhonda also baked bread, two loafs of wheat bread for David's lunch and two cinnamon loafs with raisins for breakfast. At first, Rhonda really did enjoy doing these special things for her family, but when it was demanded of her it was no longer special it now was a chore expected from her. Rhonda had enough chores. Along with weeding and picking vegetables, putting them in the freezer or canning pickles and okra and fig preserves, washing the dishes and clothes, hanging the clothes on the line, Rhonda also cut the yard with a walk behind lawn mower. Rhonda did find time to clean the house along with everything else. Rhonda was truly a countrywoman who was being controlled. Rhonda's only friends were people she met through David.

Rhonda did have her stepsister, Lily and her family, her Mom and Dad moved to SA. Rhonda's father would come and visit during the day sometimes and it would make Rhonda and Rachel's day. Rhonda became sick and could not get out of bed without throwing-up. Rhonda was six months pregnant with the second baby and Rachel needed to be watched closely. Rhonda's father came over and to Rhonda's surprise, her father washed dishes for the first time in his life. Rhonda asked, "Daddy. Where is Rachel?" Rhonda hears a dead silence. Then in a faint whisper she heard, "Oh, shit". Rhonda then heard the back screen door open and close and she turned around in the bed and saw her daddy walking down the street yelling, "Rachel, Come to Paw baby." Rachel and Jake, a black lab/Doberman mix, walked right up to Paw. Paw said, "Don't scare Paw like that any more. Don't go out the gate unless Paw or your Mom are with you. O.K.?" Daddy said, "Rachel is fine" and went back to the dishes. Rhonda did not say one word she was just relieved they were all back where they belonged.

Rhonda and her daddy were closer than ever. Rhonda's dad would pat her belly and say, "Paw loves you, little darlin". Rhonda shared everything with her Dad. Rhonda and her Dad even talked about her being unhappy with the way things were going in her marriage. Rhonda's Dad replied, "Rhonda, as long as you have a roof over your head, food in the refrigerator, and clothes on your back, and if he is not abusive hang in there as long as you can. I know it's hard but do this for Daddy." "Every thing will be alright, baby." Rhonda's Dad would visit her often and was told by her Dad that these visits were between them or May Lynn would get jealous because Dad was not visiting her daughter, Lily. I gave him my word that it would not leave the house. It did not until this moment.

Rhonda and David invited Dad and May Lynn over for supper. Rhonda's Dad loved Rhonda's cabbage supper. It was a delicious dish with Cabbage, ham, onions, potatoes, carrots, garlic, sweet basil, salt and pepper. It smelled divine. Rhonda would make corn bread with this dish and her Dad would be in hog heaven. After the supper was over May Lynn said they had to go and Rhonda was curious as to why. Rhonda asked, "Why so soon?" May Lynn replied, "Your Father's legs have been giving him trouble." May Lynn asked Rhonda not to say anything to Dad and she did not. This comment bothered Rhonda but she knew her Dad was going to the doctor. It was Halloween and the family was invited to Lily's house. Rhonda and David were getting ready and all of a sudden Rhonda heard a blood curdling scream. Rhonda ran to the kitchen and Rachel was lying on the floor with a bar stool which was missing the seat and had only a metal plate on top of her. Rachel tried to climb, what seemed to be a tower to her and she was heavy enough it toppled over on her, the metal plate hit her right between the eyes and blood was every where. Rhonda picked her up and asked David to call her physician's office and give the message to the answering service to call them back. Rhonda needed to know where to bring Rachel, and if it was to the Emergency Room, which one. Rachel's doctor called back and said he had a plastic surgeon on the way to meet us so Rachel would not have such a big scar for the rest of her life. Rhonda called May Lynn and told them what had happened. May Lynn suggested, after all was over at the hospital to come over and get Rachel's mind off of her big owee. The hospital took forever and finally all of us went in and explained what had happened. The attending physician took one look at Rhonda and said "I am sorry but you will have to wait outside the door." "I do not want to have to deliver her brother or sister tonight." Needless to say, Rhonda stood in the hall and bawled her eyes out. Everything turned out all right and you could barely see where she had hurt herself. All this and no plastic surgeon waiting, like her pediatrician said there would be.

David, Rhonda, and Rachel arrived at Dad and May Lynn's house and Paw, this is the name Rachel called Rhonda's Dad, was the first at the door to check on his girl. He took Rachel and laid her on the couch and covered her up, got her a treat and a drink and sat in the den and watched TV with her until she fell asLilyp. Paw called

MeMe, May Lynn, to get more ice for the swelling of her head and eyes. Later on that evening Rachel looked like she had two eggplants for eyes. Rachel was a good sport through all of this and her Paw made it all better.

CHAPTER 6

By now, David was set in his ways and Rhonda tried to arrange her life not to make waves of any kind. Rhonda iced down his beer two hours before he got home and had a few beers when she was not pregnant, to cope with the situation calmly. Rhonda's thoughts were always on her children. Rhonda may have had five beers through Rachel's pregnancy. David mainly stayed in the garden with his tiller and a beer. Rachel was big enough to bring him a beer now. That got pretty old for her real quick. Good for her!

The house was always in the process of being fixed. Nothing ever seemed to get finished. Never the less, David would always find something else to tear down, or into. Rhonda thought David did little projects just to give her more work than she already had. The house was always clean, floors mopped, dishes done; no electric dishwasher, yard cut and furniture dusted.

Rhonda was at her due date. Rhonda and Rachel went to the grocery store that morning and went home and put the groceries away. Rhonda asked Rachel how would she like to see her new sister or brother today? Rachel asked, "Why today, Mommy?" Rhonda replied she had been feeling contractions all morning. At two and a half, Rachel did understand after all she spent all day talking to her mommy. Rachel asked if the contractions hurt, and Rhonda would tell her no. They went out for lunch and calmed down from their busy day and it was about Rachel's naptime. The phone rang and it was her stepsister telling her Paw was taken to the hospital and all they knew was he had an aneurysm in the wall of his artery. Lily also told her,

Mc, Lilys' husband was on his way to pick her up. Rhonda got off the phone and called her Mother in Law to pick up Rachel she said she was on her way. Rhonda then called David and told him and gave him the hospital name and asked if he could meet her there. Rhonda did not tell anyone except Rachel, she had been having contractions all day.

Mc arrived at Rhonda's house and she was ready to go. She got in the car and asked if Mc heard any more about Daddy? Mc replied, No. Rhonda said a silent prayer and asked the Lord to let her reach the hospital before he took her Daddy. Before you knew it they reached the hospital and there was Gene at the front door to take Rhonda to the room the family was waiting in and she knew how much he meant to all of the family. Daddy never treated anyone of us different, Daddy show no favoritism. No one in that room could tell you one single bad thing against her Daddy. Lily and Rhonda sat together and she told her that they had already called the OB-GYN to alert him to the situation, due to the fact Rhonda was at the end of my ninth month. The Doctor,who operated on Daddy, opened the door and asked if any one would like to see Daddy before they took him. I looked at Lily and asked if she wanted to go and she said no. Rhonda wished she would have gone back but she did not. John, Rhonda's stepbrother looked at the Doctor and said no and the Doctor closed the door. Everyone stood up and gathered their things together and walked outside. Mom said she was hungry so we went to a rib place that Daddy loved. The entire family all arrived and sat at the longest table they had.

Lily was wearing a watch that had a second hand so she sat close to Rhonda. There was a chain behind Lily and Rhonda roping this one table in. As Rhonda had a contraction she would rattle the chain so Lily could time them. This went on all through supper. As we were walking out Rhonda stopped and said, "My water just broke." Mom went to the owner and explained the situation and he refused to let her use the phone. Needless to say, it did not matter how good their ribs were we would never step foot in that establishment again. Gene and David brought Rhonda to the hospital in Daddy's car, how appropriate. Rhonda was so afraid she was going to get the seat all wet. Upon arrival a nurse was at the door with a wheelchair. She explained the Doctor had called and left instructions as to what to do, he also explained the situation regarding daddy. Everyone was so nice and thoughtful.

Rhonda had been laying there for quite some time now and everyone who came in and check her status was telling her the same thing, "You are just fingertip. You have a while to go." It certainly did not feel like fingertip from her end. Lily was on her right and David on her left and they thought they were helping when they would breath with her. Not a chance, just a lot of bad-breath filling the room. All of a sudden Rhonda had her first sight, or vision. There was a foggy, drifting figure by the wall. As Rhonda looked at it she was given a sense of calmness and overwhelming love. Rhonda knew it was Daddy checking on her to see if everything was all right. Rhonda told the floating image I love you and the door opened abruptly and Rhonda was upset because she made the circle of light go away. Lily and David both went for a smoke and talked it over and came to the conclusion Rhonda was crazier than they thought. Finally the Doctor came in and said Rhonda was just fingertip and he would have to take the baby. It had been 24 hours since her water had broke. The Doctor also added her head was too large for Rhonda to pass. This was thanks to David being of big- headed German decent. Rhonda started getting suspicious when she saw three separate shifts come in and out.

To Rhonda this was the easy part. The hard part was yet to come. Daddy had a wake and the Good Lord knew exactly were to put her because she knew she could not handled it. It was sudden and a shock already on top of his new grand daughter. Rhonda was on a roller-coaster ride. Feeling of grief for her Dad and feelings of joy having a new daughter. This one threw Rhonda for a loop; trying to deal with two of the most extreme emotions at one time. Rhonda knew she was going to get visitors from people who attended the wake so the next morning she put on make up and put her hair up in a bun. Her uncle stopped by and told her what a beautiful baby girl she had and he did not mention Daddy one time. Rhonda thanked him for stopping by and asked that he please excuse me, the babys' were being brought out. Needless to say, Rhonda did not have many words for him. This was the uncle that Nannie and Rhonda lived in his back yard. Rhonda still had ill feeling of him. She as nice for my Daddy's sake.

It came time to take the bundle of joy home and start the routine over again. Rhonda put the tragic event on hold never forgetting just on hold. This was Rhonda's private hell, no one else would know.

Mom was not sure if she could handle Salien, but she invited the family to stay with her for a week. David and Rhonda and Rachel and brand new Salien, stayed with Rhonda'a mom who helped her for a while. In spite of the situation, Mom embraced her new grandbaby girl and loved her just like all the others.

CHAPTER 7

As time went on the girls grew up quickly. They were always busy playing house or mud pies or swinging each other in the swing. After the girls would eat lunch then it would be lesson time. The girls knew how to say and write their ABC's. They knew their colors and numbers. After lesson time the girls would take a nap.

This was the best time of their life. To get them ready for Kindergarten, Rhonda found a Baptist church that offered Pre-School for 3-5 year olds. Rachel went first and Salien followed. The girls only went for 3 hours a day and this was a full day for those little ones. Rhonda was always their waiting for them along with all the other mothers. When Rhonda and the girls arrived home they would want a snack and a nap. When they got up they were ready to go again.

Rhonda was doing laundry and she and the girls went outside to the laundry room. As usual Rhonda opened the washer and then put her arm in and pulled out the clothes to hang on the line. On this sunny day there was a friend of the family who owned a big trailer and front loader. He was in the back pasture clearing out the creek bed of trees. Rhonda happened to look inside the washer and she saw a diamond pattern, looked like a belt or leather she was not sure then she saw it move. Rhonda eased her arm out of the washer and told the girls to go to the back door. Rhonda ran to the back door opened it and the girls followed yelling, "What's the matter Mommy?" Rhonda did not answer them she was in her own thoughts on getting the friend, 15 acres back, to the front to help her. Rhonda grabbed a mirror that was hanging in the hall. She and the girls ran back outside and Rhonda started to flash the light of the sun towards the front loader and sure enough her friend came to her rescue. Rhonda explained what she had seen in the washer and Thorn, the friend, had a heavy pair of leather gloves. Rhonda took the girls and stood back away from the washer, and still not answering their question, flying above their heads was a 4-foot bull snake. Rhonda had a pool hose for a drain on her washing machine so she could water the grass and the trees in the summer. The snake must have found the hose and crawled into the washing machine and got a bath. Thorn took the bull snake and put it back in the acres he had already cleared. First he explained to the girls the bull snake imitates a rattlesnake. The bull snake will whip it's tail fast to sound like a rattler, and it even looks like a rattler, at a quick glance.

The girls were growing by leaps and bounds. Soon they were playing games on TV. Rhonda kept a look out for David to pull up in the driveway so the girls could turn their game off. David thought they should be weeding or doing something constructive since he worked all day. This got worse as the girls got older. Soon there was no work in town so the family had to pack up and move to Atlanta, Georgia for 2 years. The girls made new friends and excelled in school. Salien was in accelerated classes and Rachel was doing better than she was before. On this move the family encountered a friend from home and his family. Walt followed us to Atlanta, Georgia and lived fairly close to us. Walt ended up getting fired by David and then David got him back on the job with a promise to do much better. With too many family problems Walt packed his family up and headed home.

David called an old friend who was getting up in years to come and help him. Mr. Joe agreed to come up and was assured by David his expenses would be taken care of. All of us went to bed that evening and Rhonda had her second premonition. Rhonda's premonitions started coming to her in her dreams. These dreams were very vivid as if she were there standing in the background watching every step of each person involved. The next morning everyone woke up and the girls got ready for school, and David was ready for work. Rhonda asked him to hang back for a minute. Rhonda told David, "If Mr. Joe comes here he is going to die."

David asked, "Did you have a dream?" She answered, "Yes. The phone is going to ring in the evening and it is going to be Joe. He is going to ask for you. I will ask him if he is OK? Mr. Joe will say yes but I really need David. Rhonda then hands the phone to David and you talk for a second and you're out the door. When you pull up at the Hotel you will see an ambulance at Joe's door parked parallel to his room. The paramedics will be working on Joe. He is having a heart attack and he will not make it out of the room. You will come home and look at me and say, "He's gone." We have to call his family and make arrangements to get the body back to Texas. Needless to say, it happened just as Rhonda explained it to David. It was Christmas time and the girls were looking at the tree in the living room. Salien went to Rhonda and said, "Mommy, I just saw Mr. Joe in the living room walking around." Rhonda told Salien, he's just checking on us, it's OK he won't hurt you. Salien went to bed and took it as it was a normal thing.

CHAPTER 8

T he time was over in Georgia and we moved on to North Carolina. The girls saw a good snow for the first time. Their eyes were as big as silver dollars. Snow angels were everywhere in the yard. The girls had a blast sliding down the long hillsides. Rhonda was busy taking basics in college. That was a challenge. The house had a basement the length of the house. The girls would invite their friends to come over and bring their skates and use the basement as a skating ring.

Rhonda felt this was the most normal time her children ever had in their lifetime. They had a beautiful two-story home, making friends and having them over, playing out side and did not want to come in for supper they were having so much fun. Rhonda wished she could have bottled this feeling for them for life. After two years the family returned home to Texas. There were renters in our home, so Rhonda's family had to resort to renting once again.

Naturally everyone who followed the family for work to Atlanta and North Carolina followed us home. One in particular was arren and his wife Levi and their three children. After about a year or two back Rachel started babysitting for Darren and Levi. Rhonda thought everything was going well until Rhonda noticed Rachel acting withdrawn, sad, troubled but would not talk to Rhonda about the problem. As a concerned Mom, Rhonda went through Rachel's drawers to see if their would be an answer a clue as to what was troubling Rachel. Rhonda found a letter begging Darren to quit, please quit having sex with her. This was the answer every mother feared; her father's best friend was molesting her daughter. It came to light when Rachel and her father, David came home. David's reaction was not for his daughter's well being but that of his friend's reputation. Rhonda almost fell out of her chair. Rhonda spoke up and before she knew it on the open fire of the gas stove where David was standing, in went the letter. The only hard-core hand written evidence that Darren was guilty for what he was doing to their daughter. Poor Salien knew, saw and probably sworn to secrecy with her life. This was the day Rhonda was feeling so sorry and sick at the same time for both of her girls; to have to go through this at fourteen and twelve. When all was said and done, the court date was set. Rhonda was there with David, Rachel and Salien. David needed to know this was real. Rachel needed to have closure. Salien needed to know first her sister was going to be OK and it was all right to tell the truth when someone is being hurt.

Rhonda simply lost her little girl over night. Rhonda was heartbroken but stood firm for her family, her girls.

CHAPTER 9

It was not long after Rachel's incident Rhonda's Mom found out she had lung cancer and the doctor gave her 6 months to live. At first, Lily took care of Mom and worked. The last 2 months Rhonda moved in with her Mom and Lily to help and be there 24 hours a day and 7 days a week. Rhonda saw to it that Mom got what ever she wanted to eat, drink or do. Rhonda also had control of Mom's medication and oxygen machine. Mom would look over at Lily and Rhonda and say, "Let's go be bad!" Rhonda would take the oxygen off Mom and help her up and out the door we went to her chair out side and Rhonda light her Mom's cigarette. Rhonda lost Mom on Christmas night at 9:10 p.m.

Since Rhonda moved out of her house, she became more and more aware of how unhappy she was and it was not at all healthy for her girls. Rhonda gave it the ole' college try and it lasted eleven days. It was the morning the flying mattress across the room that gave her the shove, no pun intended, to confront David and tell him to get out and do not come back. Rhonda must have made her point because he left, as she required. Of course there were words, but she was quite proud of the outcome.

Divorce proceedings began immediately. It took three months, which seemed like eternity, to end. Rhonda had her two girls with her and a house and almost one acre of the 13 that was David's and his mothers. Rhonda was beside her self. Free at last, was the phrase of the day and weeks to come.

July 4th was near and Rhonda was at home chilling out with a cold beverage and a knock at the door was heard. Rhonda answered the door and it was Rachel's boyfriends mom asking her to take a ride with her to find someone. At first Rhonda said, "No". Persistent she was and Rhonda ended up in the van. Boyfriend's Mom went one way and Rhonda another. Rhonda was approached by a gentleman who asked her to dance. OK. What harm can come from a dance she thought.

Rhonda made the biggest mistake of her life she married a preditor. Kevin was his name and he was charming, handsome and a gentleman. Rhonda should have known from that it was to good to be true. But she thought, could this be what she's been waiting for all of her life? The answer is impeccably NO! Kevin poured out the charm, hugs, kisses, and compliments, all the things she was starved of for eighteen years. Rhonda's head was spinning like a top. She thought she found heaven and Kevin was it. The girls did not approve, this was red flag number two. Rhonda was so overwhelmed with the feeling of being noticed and given warm feelings she only thought of herself and not that of her girls. Big Red Flag, one that still haunts her to this very day. Although she has managed to forgive she never forgets.

Kevin brought back pot into Rhonda's life and then speed. This went on for four years. Kevin and Rhonda took out loans on the house for upgrading and half of each loan was given to Kevin who paid all his back bills with the money. This was done three times. There was cheating of course and his ex was calling nightly for a while until Rhonda put her foot down and said it's her or me.

Too bad it was not her.

Kevin and Rhonda went on as a couple, and bought a pontoon boat. The girls liked the boat when Kevin would invite them. Can't forget hunting in the back yard. Rhonda's dogs gained at least ten pounds on unfound dead doves in the back yard. Rhonda could go on and on but she will spare you the, "been there done that", routine.

Rhonda received a visit at work from Saline, who was obviously upset. Rhonda's boss at the time walked outside with us. Saline told

Rhonda, Rachel had been shot. Rhonda ask what hospital was she in and we would bring her home and take care of her. The whole time Rhonda was talking Saline was shaking all over and her head was nodding no, no no Momma. She is dead! Rhonda screamed NNNNNNNNNNNOOOOOOOOO. Her first words were who did this to her and Saline said Mario, Rachel's boyfriend, 20 years her senior. He shot her in the back with a sawed-off shotgun at point blank range. Rhonda should have consoled her Saline but instead Rhonda fell to her knees and cried like a baby. Rhonda asked Saline, "Where is he?" Saline told her, "In jail". It did not seem real. Rhonda had just seen Rachel 2 months before and she was angry Rhonda for making her man friend move a trailer out of her yard. If looks could kill Rhonda would have been gone. Rhonda's first born, dead. Rhonda could not comprehend that Saline was there at work and told her what she just heard.

Rhonda was relieved from work for 2 weeks and Kevin came and took Rhonda home. Not a word was spoken. Rhonda went inside and she immediately got herself, Kevin and Saline a beer. Just what the family needed at that time. Again Rhonda was selfish and only thought of her loss and not that of Saline. Rhonda asked Saline, "Why didn't your father stop this from happening?" Saline did not have an answer.

The neighbors came over and Rhonda told them what had happen. They stayed with her almost all day. Plans where made to go where Rachel's body was being held and the next day Kevin and Rhonda all drove up and got a hotel room. When Rhonda inquired as to the whereabouts of Rachel's body, she was told her father moved her to another funeral home. Rhonda now had to find Rachel's body because her father would not tell her where she was. By this time Rachel was already cremated.

When Rhonda found Rachel and explained she was her Mother, Rhonda was brought to a room with 2 chairs and 2 couches. Rhonda sat on the couch and Kevin sat on the opposite one. The door opened and a lady came into the room holding a blue box with a blue ribbon around it. It was Rachel's ashes, still hot. Rhonda was in a nightmare not at her daughter's funeral. Rachel deserved so much better. Rhonda did not get a chance to say good-bye, kiss her on her cheek or hold her hand. Rhonda was handed a hot blue box and told this is Rachel's ashes.

Between Kevin and the ex, Rhonda did not know if she was coming or going. Kevin, Saline and Rhonda went to a bay where Rachel caught her first big red fish. Again this was all planned by her father, but he did remember to tell the man of the cloth not to mention her mother as a survivor. After a few words from the man of the cloth, Rachel's dad and sister scattered her ashes in the bay. No one ask if Rhonda wanted to save some for an urn. It was as if Rhonda did not exist. From Rachel's fathers outlook he was punishing Rhonda for remarrying.

This is when the PTSD really started to show. Rhonda was angry all the time. Rhonda did not want to do anything outside of work but go home. Rhonda started drinking more than usual. She did not care about anything or anybody. Rhonda went into a shell and she knew she needed to stay there for her sanity. This is when Rhonda should have gotten help from a counselor and did not. Rhonda desperately needed help and guidance. All of the pain from the loss of Rachel began to cascade like a waterfall. The guilt from marring such a creep that kept her away from her girls flooded her thoughts. This was differently time for intervention.

Not only was Rhonda's mental state very fragile, her health was not doing well, she learned she had RA, Hep C, and she was on the verge of a heart attack which ended with a stint in her RCA, high blood pressure and over all depression. Then came rupture of a disc in her back and after surgery she learned she had Degenerative disc disease. More surgery this time on the neck with a titanium plate screwed in. Rhonda had to file for disability. The pain grew each day and some day's it was unbearable. Rhonda then learned why her back was hurting so much, she has 7 herniated disc.

The marriage broke up. Rhonda lost her job. She almost lost her home.

It wasn't until after Rhonda sold the house where the girls grew up that she sought therapy. Rhonda is still in therapy today with a wonderful counselor, and also a psychiatrist. Rhonda will continue to do so until she is to the point she can handle her affairs more clearly. Thank God for both of them. Rhonda would not be here without her Earth's hidden angel's help.

CHAPTER 10

After the divorce Rhonda was forced to move. The house she lived in for twenty- nine years was going to be foreclosed on. Rhonda did some thinking and put the house up for sale. Rhonda sold the house and moved into and apartment.

In the prelude Sergeant James was introduced. While Rhonda was in therapy she met Sergeant James and he agreed to speak with her concerning his PTSD.

Sergeant James spent eight (8) years in the military. Here is his story.

Soldier's give their lives and limbs defending the United States of America and the fortunate ones who come home deserve respect and gratitude from us, civilians, for there heroic efforts.

Unfortunately, some do come home with an illness called Post Traumatic Stress Disorder, ie PTSD. The severity of the illness varies from one to another. The PTSD is an illness, not unlike strep throat and chicken pox. Our soldiers with PTSD should not be shunned or used as scapegoats when tragedy strikes after returning home.

The one thing we have discovered is therapy, talking to someone, is a great help. Also there are medications, which can be administered by psychiatrist that also help. Another therapy is a pet, be it dog, cat, lizard, snake. During one of Rhonda's own therapy groups, she met an intelligent young man who has PTSD as Rhonda does.

Born into a loving family, his Mother and Father adored their only son. Sergeant James grew up as a normal boy, playing base- ball, football, and softball. Almost to the point of being spoiled, Sergeant James always maintained manners and a very concerning heart for others.

His first tour of duty was Afghanistan. Total, Sergeant James gave 8 eight years to the Army; the first 2 two years were in the field as a communications officer. This is where the PTSD began.

Sergeant James was receiving radio communications for the team's next destination. Shooting started from afar and his Captain Luke gave the order to stop. Captain Luke stepped out of the humvee and went to the front and tragically, Captain Luke stepped on an IED. Blood and body parts shattered the humvee. The humvee turned over quickly and threw Sergeant James out. As he turned back towards the humvee to see if his brothers of the team were all right, Tom the driver turned his head and his eye was dangling in blood on his cheek. John, the gunner, was now in the back of the humvee sat up and screamed "my arm." When John got free he rolled out of the humvee carrying his mangled arm and bLilyding profusely.

At this point James became numb. Totally numb.

This began the PTSD. Sergeant James never saw such a sight in his life. He was aware that he would see this, just did not think it would be his unit and so quickly. From that moment on he walked with a straight face, expressionless, as he shot to kill anything or anybody. This went on for two years in different places but all similar horrific scenes of blood, guts, body parts but no glory.

Sergeant James dealt with his anger by pushing all this to the back of his brain waiting, almost like putting books on a shelf to read at a later date. The difference here was too many books, which had already gathered dust before he could put it on his shelf in his mind.

Sergeant James received a Purple Heart for being wounded, a Silver Medal for Courage under fire and two Bronze Medals in which he helped to achieve his objectives as a soldier.

Ironically, Sergeant James was now turning civilians into killers while serving in the reserves. Showing them what to look for and how and when to move. He also showed the recruits how to determine the land and disarm the bombs. Showing each one how the different types of firearms worked.

Sergeant James was always aware of his surroundings as he was trained to do and teaching others the same. When discharged Sergeant James found it very difficult to shut down these actions. He also realized the dust was clearing off the metaphoric books and no one understood the night sweats and outburst at night the sudden snap of his head looking where the loud noise came from. Sergeant James was trained to shoot without giving it a thought. He was trained to protect not only his life but also the lives of his "Brothers".

There is help for both civilians and a soldier returning home and it is therapy. Please talk to someone who can help you sort through this illness. Your hidden angel is waiting to help!

The End

FROM THE AUTHOR

PTSD is very dear to my heart. I heard on the T.V. that two soldiers blew their brains out at home with their wives in the other room. One had a brand new baby girl. This broke my heart. If this book helps just one person I will be happy. I have been diagnosed with it for 5 years, I am still in therapy, and proud to say so. I have never learned so much about myself until I started therapy.

The military men and women need the same for PTSD. If it is not the member then it will be a therapist or a psychiatrist. Someone will answer the phone to speak with you and you will not have to wait two hours to speak to someone.

The civilians at home will not forget you and you do have someone to talk to always, most importantly someone who cares.

About the Author

J anice Bell was diagnosed seven years ago with Post Tramatic Stress Disorder. She started treatment and still to this day is in theropy every 3 months.

Janice resides inTexas. She loves cooking and being with her family and animals also writes poetry.

Janice also loves gardening.

www.ingramcontent.com/pod-product-compliance
Lightning Source LLC
Chambersburg PA
CBHW020357290526
45785CB00005B/2326